Mindfulness for beginners

Mindfulness for Beginners

A Practical Guide to Finding
Peace and Happiness
in an Anxious World

Graham Cann

Dedicated to my wonderful wife
Jules
with all my love

Contents

INTRODUCTION

*"What lies behind us and what lies before us are tiny matters
compared to what lies within us"*
RALPH WALDO EMERSON

I believe that buying this book could be one of the most inspired decisions you have ever made.

You have chosen to look into what is a proven route to achieving lasting peace and happiness. The effect of a full-on immersion in mindfulness will be something that your future self will thank you for. How amazing it will be when you can not only remain calm and contented in the normal day-to-day routines of your life, but also even in the most trying of circumstances.

Wherever you go in life and whatever you do, there can be no argument about the fact that **you** will always be there, carrying with you your beliefs, values and internal dialogue that can be either empowering or disempowering.

When your thoughts and your beliefs are disempowering, you will experience an unhappiness with yourself, your job, your relationships and your life in general. Some solutions to these circumstances can lead to even greater problems in the long run in the form of drug and alcohol dependency and failing mental health.

Many people are under the illusion that moving to a different place within their own country or overseas will somehow see them metamorphise into a different person, a more contented version of their current self. Starting a new business or changing partners are often seen as a route that will somehow have the same effect. It doesn't take too long before people come to terms with the reality that life doesn't work like that.

If you're an anxious worrier now, then no amount of superficial external change will transform you into a happier, more confident human being. A deeper work needs to take place – a work that begins to change you from the inside out.

That is where an understanding of mindfulness comes in. It can be a truly transformational experience. This book has been designed for someone with little or no knowledge of the subject and take them on a journey of discovery. A journey normally has a starting point and concludes at a destination. Mindfulness, however, provides a continuous revelation throughout life and the results, generally speaking, will depend on how committed you are to the process. As in any activity where there is a requirement to change your habits, a wholehearted response is more likely to have the desired outcome.

I look forward to taking you step-by-step along this new route, understanding that you may be tentative about setting off but I'll be mapping out where you need to travel. I'll be pointing out any loose boulders that could cause you to trip up and fall. You'll be joining the thousands of folk who have taken the same road before you. They have actually reached that new place that you may have only dreamt of going to - the place where happiness and contentment does indeed reside within and you won't have to literally move away to achieve it!

1. WHAT IS MINDFULNESS?

"You are the sky. Everything else is just the weather"
PEMA CHODRON

Mindfulness has its origins in ancient Eastern meditation practices of religious and spiritual institutions namely Hinduism and Buddhism but not solely these. Mindfulness is also rooted in Islam, Judaism and Christianity. The popularity of Mindfulness in the West has been prompted more by secular institutions and individuals.

Jon Kabat-Zinn founded the Mindfulness-Based Stress Reduction (MBSR) programme at the University of Massachusetts Medical School in 1979 to treat the chronically ill. He is seen as the main individual who brought the whole concept of Mindfulness to a Western world which was having its challenges with rising rates of anxiety and depression.

In the same way that yoga spread to the West via eastern religions, so Mindfulness has followed and indeed, both Mindfulness and yoga are similar in so far as each discipline is concerned with the awareness of one's body.

In a world where there have been amazing technological leaps forward, we're all living longer thanks to medical discoveries; people can fly around the world and visit countries hitherto out of reach; we have access to the most incredible information online; Man has walked on the moon and continues to venture forth in space travel; we can video-call relations on the other side of the world; for most of us in the West we have food to put on the table, but, for all this, we continue to see mental health problems rise around the world.

Despite having relatively prosperous lifestyles compared to vast swathes of the world's population, cracks have been showing for many years. In the UK, the amount of people reporting mental health problems has risen by 20% between 1993 and 2014 in both men and women. Cases of self-harm and those who have had suicidal thoughts are alarmingly high with suicides on the increase especially among young men. There is an underlying tension in the lives of everyday people.   Life is not as rosy as one would expect. To make matters worse, the global pandemic of 2020 has multiplied the problem.

It is more important than ever in today's full-on, hectic, target-driven world that we start realising that despite the stress and anxiety of modern day living, we can, if we choose to, find that calm oasis. The place where we're able to connect to the present moment and within a few minutes feel less tension and less pressure and feel more able to cope again.

So with cases of mental illness rising and mental health provision in dire need, it is down to each one of us to find answers nearer to home, solutions that we can come up with that will start to reverse this trend. One such way is to begin your own Mindfulness journey. Even if we consider ourselves as not being overtly troubled by worry and stress, the charity Mind states that 1 in 4 of us will experience some kind of mental health problem.

Daily mindfulness practice will begin to help us cope when those awkward, difficult, stress-induced challenges occur. We will just feel more able to deal with whatever life throws at us.

As with all new practices and habits, it is said to take 60 days for our minds to accept any new habit without fighting against it. As we shall see later on, our subconscious minds are programmed to maintain the status quo which requires no effort whatsoever and which will clearly change nothing. To paraphrase Henry Ford - if we carry on doing what we've always done, we'll always get what we've always got.

Mindfulness is the complete opposite of being mind-full.

How often are our minds crammed with so many pressing thoughts that we fail to hear the melodic robin singing from the rose bush; the rustling of the wind in the trees goes unnoticed; we miss the stunning fragrance from a honeysuckle bush and the bright, life giving sun on our exposed flesh does not register with us at all. There is so much going on around us every second of every day if only we allow ourselves to let go - letting go of all those thoughts which compete for our attention all day, every day. Let them go in favour of the present moment, the 'now'.

There is a power in that simple step. By simple, I mean a simple concept. It can take time to reach the place where you begin to access the power of love, joy, happiness and peace that resides within each one of us and which is accessible in the stillness of life

Kabat-Zinn describes mindfulness as "the awareness that arises from paying attention, on purpose, in the present moment and non-judgmentally". It is easy to see how non-judgmental reflection can be a healthy alternative in the age of social media where commentary, likes and opinions are not in short supply. We are constantly judging others in so far as what they are wearing, how they speak, their opinions, what they look like, their mannerisms and so on. Let's not forget also how much we're inclined to judge ourselves.

Mindfulness is learning to live in the present moment being aware of our five senses as we go about our daily lives. In a way, it's opting out of autopilot, making ourselves notice our immediate environment and becoming more attuned to it. It is a daily practice as we travel to and from work, carry out everyday chores such as cleaning, washing up, going for a walk, changing the baby or meeting a friend for a coffee.

We can practice mindfulness anytime and anywhere by being engaged with the present moment. Many of us go about our lives on autopilot and filling our minds with thoughts or sensations that are either connected to past activity (regret mode) or with something coming up in the future (worry mode).

A recent Harvard study showed that nearly 50% of people spend their waking hours thinking about something unconnected with what they were doing. Researchers concluded that a wandering mind is an unhappy mind.

When it comes to learning something new like mindfulness, knowledge is **not** power. The only power it has is when you put that knowledge into action. So to obtain the greatest benefit from mindfulness, it needs to be practised regularly for maximum effect. We'll be looking at how mindfulness works, how it will benefit you and then go on to look at a number of exercises that you can practice at home, at work and in the great outdoors.

How does mindfulness differ from meditation? They can overlap but they are not exactly the same. Meditation normally refers to a formal, intentional seated practice and can take a number of different forms from mantra-based meditation to guided meditation.

So whereas meditation is generally practised for a set period of time, mindfulness practice can be applied at any time of the day. You can, of course, combine regular meditation within your mindfulness routine. Mindfulness meditation can last anything from five minutes up to half an hour or more in duration. As a beginner, practice this for five minutes and then increase this time as the weeks and months go by.

Mindfulness is more of a lifestyle where you're paying attention and being present in whatever you're doing, taking notice of your five senses, your feelings and behaviours.

As we embark on this journey together, begin to become more aware of the present moment using your five senses. Right now, wherever you are and whatever you're doing, stop and consider:

What can you hear? What sounds do you hear? There may be many sounds or just one?

What can you see? Concentrate on any object that is in front of you right now. Look closely at the object for a few minutes and taking in all that you notice like the shape of it, the colour, the pattern, without judgment. If any thoughts come into your mind while you're doing this, be aware of them and then let them go and bring your focus back on to the object. Try this now for a couple of minutes.

Is there any odour that you can smell, fragrant or otherwise?

If you're eating, how does it taste? What does it feel like in your mouth?

Whatever it is you are touching, what does it feel like? Is it rough or smooth?

The goal of this exercise is to give you a basic introduction to how mindfulness works. By doing this practice, you will have turned off your mind's incessant chatter and given yourself a break from your conscious mind talk. This can lead in the longer term to a significant source of mental refreshment.

Why is this important?

Because the present moment is the only place where you can be fully alive.

2. IT'S ALL IN THE HEAD

"Our life is shaped by our mind, for we become what we think"
BUDDHA

Imagine that we have a computer inside our heads. Our brain is the hardware. It contains connections, wiring, storage, memory and processing power needed by us to function as human beings.

Our mind is the software – the operating system that gathers, stores and manages information using the huge processing capability of the brain. The brain and the mind are interconnected. One cannot operate without the other.

Our brain contains 100 billion nerve cells or neurons. In terms of 100 billion grains of sand, that's enough to fill two baths. These nerve cells transmit and receive thoughts, emotions, actions and the automatic processes of our bodies.

Whilst we don't know everything about the mind and how it operates, what is known is that there is a conscious and a subconscious mind. The conscious mind accounts for around 10% of its total operating power. Its job is to identify information coming in from our five senses – sight, sound, smell, taste and touch. It makes decisions, finds patterns, makes comparisons and controls our short-term memories.

This leaves a whopping 90% of operating power in the subconscious mind. This is hugely powerful and yet we may not even be aware of it on a conscious level. This part of our mind includes running areas of our bodies like breathing, sleeping and our heart rate. It stores and retrieves long-term memories, causes us to go into a fight or flight response when facing danger, creates and maintains habits and prefers to maintain the status quo rather than facing any change that we might want to implement. It is not rational and cannot distinguish between right or wrong, good or bad. **The**

subconscious mind just accepts what it is told whether it's true or not. We then go about our lives thinking, feeling and behaving in ways that confirm that 'truth'.

We can immediately see how incredibly important it is to speak positive words over our lives and not phrases like 'I'm useless' or 'I'll never understand that' because the subconscious mind will believe whatever you tell it.

In order to see clearly how a certain situation pans out in the mind, imagine we're walking along the pavement, we decide to cross the street and step off the kerb. We're aware of the sound of a car engine. We turn round to face the direction of the moving car to identify the sound. This is the first function.

The second function is to compare. The information we have about the car goes to the subconscious mind that has stored all the information we've ever experienced about moving cars. This will depend on whether the car is doing 30 miles an hour and is 500 yards away in which case it's safe to cross. Alternatively, if the car's doing 60 miles an hour and only 100 yards away, we'll receive a danger signal.

The third function of our conscious mind is analysis followed by the fourth function, deciding.

So understanding how the subconscious mind works helps us in our quest to change our habits. If we want to form a new habit like mindfulness meditation we now know that the subconscious mind will resist this move. This is natural and to be expected every time we want to change anything in our lives. We'll feel uncomfortable until the new habit has been accepted by the subconscious mind when the new habit itself will then become part of the status quo.

As a footnote, the thing about habits is that they can be truly empowering and beneficial on the one hand but on the other, many of us live with habits that are disempowering. We carry on with these routines because we've always done them and much of the time, we don't even realise how much of a hold they have on us. It is a good idea to analyse our habits, looking out for the more destructive ones and forming a new habit to break the old one.

3. THE UNQUIET MIND

"You either control your mind or
it controls **you**"
NAPOLEON HILL

To fully understand mindfulness, we need to look at the power of thinking. As human beings, it's something we do incessantly. In fact, experts believe that in the course of one day, your mind has to cope with 50,000 thoughts or around 2,100 thoughts in an hour.

Not only are there thousands of thoughts whizzing around our brains on an hourly basis vying for attention, but also what those thoughts are communicating to us all the time over and over again, often reinforcing negativity - "I'll never amount to anything", "I'm simply not good enough", "I'm an idiot", "I haven't got the patience'.

Thoughts are not facts.

We are what we **think** we are and very rarely is that a positive interpretation. In the end, what can happen is that an erroneous thought can become a belief. That unshakeable belief is now something that we truly feel about ourselves although, in reality, it may have no truth in it whatsoever. How many people are living this kind of lie? What if we have believed something negative about ourselves for 5, 10, 20 or even over 50 years and it actually isn't true at all? This is not at all uncommon. But I digress……

Imagine the scenario of being in the kitchen doing the washing up while your partner is in the garden cutting the grass. As you're fully engaged in this activity, the lawn mower starts up and your focus now drifts to your partner in the garden. That person now comes to mind and you're wondering if they remembered to put pasta on the shopping list as you'd asked them to do. You may now remember that you're short of potatoes and they should have been put on the list too. Indeed, where is the shopping list? You can't remember where it is so you leave the task and are now furiously rummaging around for it.

What has happened now is that from being fully engaged in one single activity, one thought has led to another which has led to yet another. You are no longer living in the present moment but have now drifted into thinking about the past and the future. Your mind can only hold one thought at a time but typically, when the mind begins to wander, thoughts generate further thoughts and this continues unless we direct our focus somewhere else. Being mindful, we're able to redirect our attention to the task in hand. The quality of being present and fully immersed in what we're doing right now means that we keep our mind on that single task until it's completed without going on a mental wild goose chase. Whenever competing thoughts or sensations come into our heads, we observe them without judgment and let them go.

Physiological symptoms are often influenced by the mind and the emotions, rather than a definite bodily cause like an injury. This is known as psychosomatic.

21

Illness of this type can be triggered by emotional stress and manifest itself as physical pain and other symptoms. Other types of psychosomatic disorders resulting from stress include respiratory problems, hypertension, migraine and tension headaches, gastrointestinal disturbances, impotence, frigidity, ulcers and dermatitis. So getting control of our minds will not only result in a more peaceful day-to-day existence but also may start dealing with physical ailments that plague so many people today.

THE EGO

Among the many reasons for having an unquiet mind is this little agent provocateur, the ego. It can create a tension in us that does not bode well as we strive towards adopting a more peaceful and centred state. Embracing our true self and denying the ego is a central part of Buddhism and other spiritual practices.

So what is the ego? This is Ekhart Tolle's great description of it in his book 'A New Earth':

"An ego that wants something from another – and what ego doesn't – will usually play some kind of role to get its 'needs' met, be they material gain, a sense of power, superiority, or specialness, or some kind of gratification, be it physical or psychological. Usually people are completely unaware of the roles they play. They are the roles. Some roles are subtle; others are blatantly obvious, except to the person playing it. Some roles are designed simply to get attention from others. The ego thrives on others' attention…such as recognition, praise, admiration, or just to be noticed in some way, to have its existence acknowledged."

The ego keeps us enslaved without being aware of it. It is like an intruder, this false self, who is never happy with what we have and causes us to become anxious or even depressed when we aren't striving towards our next goal or object of desire. The ego feels very comfortable in the past – how we've been wronged by someone, what we should have said to someone but didn't, how we failed at something. It's also comfortable in the future – the next holiday, that dream house or big car.

Unknown to us, we start playing roles that don't reflect our **true** selves. Roles that are predominantly occupied with survival, accumulation and wealth while, at the same time, building an identity that sets us above other people and helps us to be accepted.

Take a look at the behaviours below. Each one is fuelled by the ego in its effort to satisfy the need for attention and desire for fulfilment:

> People pleasing or demanding/needing respect
> Materialism and greed
> Dissatisfaction with what we have
> Superiority and prejudice
> Defensive actions
> Vanity or self-hatred
> Judgments and opinions
> Complaining, bitterness and resentment
> Competition, a need to control others
> Need to be in control
> Black and white thinking

What the ego hates is the present moment.

People possessed by the ego live as if the present moment is their enemy; they don't want to be who they're with; they're doing something but want to be at the end of their doing; they don't want to be where they are; they want to be somewhere else – always striving away from the present moment.

As Tolle says "All that is required to become free of the ego is to be aware of it, since awareness and ego are incompatible. Awareness is the power that is concealed in the present moment".

This is where mindfulness is an incredibly powerful tool. Every time our minds slip into the past or the future, we can train it to come back to the present moment concentrating our thinking on our immediate surroundings whatever we're doing, wherever we are.

4. THE NINE MINDFUL ATTITUDES

"Mindfulness is a way of befriending ourselves and our experience"
JON KABAT-ZINN

LIVING IN THE FAST LANE

We live in a fast-paced society. We're all trying to cram into each day more and more with very few moments where we can actually take a break and appreciate what's happening around us. Mornings are often frenetic. We're eating breakfast, jotting down the shopping list and listening to the radio all at the same time.   Then there's checking the children have everything they need for school.

The children have to be dropped off and the dog needs its morning walk while all the time thinking how we're going to explain to our mother-in-law that she can't come over next week because of a double booking. Train or bus journeys to work are not exempt from our 'doing' mode – out comes the laptop checking pending work issues or the mobile phone is deployed to check social media sites. Paranoia starts to surface when we didn't get the number of 'likes' we expected on our last post or, worse, someone has posted an obnoxious rant criticising us for no reason, raising our heart rate and anxiety levels. And so the day progresses in a similar vein.

In the rush to accomplish all these tasks, we've actually lost connection with the present moment, or being fully immersed in what we're doing and how we're feeling at any given moment. Many of the tasks are done with mindless repetition.

It is estimated that the average adult makes around 35,000 decisions on a daily basis. Our brains can't consider every one of them. For example, we don't have to remember to get dressed every day. Our mind has automated decision-making equipment to save energy and allow our conscious mind to work on more taxing activities.

THERE WILL ALWAYS BE CLOUDS IN THE SKY

One day we look up into the sky and it's filled with dark, ominous looking clouds. There is no escaping the fact that a storm is on the way and, indeed, it does come with lashing rain, strong gales and a thunder and lightning display that makes us fearful and anxious about whether the storm will cause widespread damage like uprooting trees and taking tiles from our roof.

Fast forward to the next day and the sun is casting its light and warmth over our locality. The storm has subsided, the sky is blue and there's not a hint of wind in the atmosphere. There is not a cloud in the sky.

Nothing is permanent in this world – everything comes and goes in its own time. One thing we can absolutely be sure of in life is change. All things will pass. Problems and difficulties in our lives are not permanent. Enjoyable times are also subject to change which makes it important to make the most of every second in the present moment. Mindfulness helps us to **not** hang on or get attached to emotions, thoughts, events. They all pass away.

Let's now take a look at what are considered to be the nine attitudes of mindfulness:

1. IT IS WHAT IT IS

When we look at what has happened in our lives and what is happening now, we need to look at these things with a sense of acceptance. Whatever it is you're feeling at any time, accept that feeling without any resistance.

Accepting what's already happened in our lives means that we know we cannot change what's happened. What would be the point of resisting what already is?

Of course, that doesn't mean we're unable to do anything about what is happening now. Instead of reacting to something, like taking an impulsive and opposite action, accept it for what it is. Once you've done that, you're then in a position to respond to it by, for instance, acting thoughtfully and more favourably.

James Baraz puts it succinctly when he says: "Mindfulness is simply being aware of what is happening right now without wishing it were different; enjoying the pleasant without holding on when it changes (which it will); being with the unpleasant without fearing it will always be this way (which it won't)".

Resistance and wanting for things to be other than what they are, can lead to stress and anxiety. Acceptance brings calmness and it happens **in the moment.**

2. BEING NON-JUDGMENTAL

We've already touched on this earlier. A good mental challenge is to see how many times that we are judgmental in the course of one day. It could be judging the look on someone's face; the sound of someone's voice; the choice of your partner's TV programme; whether something is fair or unfair, beautiful or ugly.

Believe me, you'll be surprised how often we make these judgments.

From a mindfulness perspective, it's all about just experiencing or observing. There's no need to give any meaning to other people's actions or, for that matter, our own thoughts, feelings and actions. It's only when we give thoughts to things that they take on any meaning at all.

During mindfulness exercises it's easy to criticise ourselves for letting our minds wander off and start engaging with our thoughts. It is important not to do so. Engendering a love and acceptance of ourselves in spite of our imperfections is essential to maintain good mental health. If it happens, accept it, let go of the thought and return your mind to what you are focusing on.

3. SEEING THE WORLD ANEW

Adopt a willingness to see things and people with a new curiosity and vitality. Be engaged and present with our friends and loved ones in a way that jettisons all those preconceived ideas and judgments we hold.

As we hold a leaf in our hand as if for the very first time, feel its texture, look at the lines of the veins in the leaf and any imperfections. See everything from the perspective of someone new to this planet. Nurture a sense of wonder and awe.

4. LETTING GO

Allowing things to be as they are without the need to control our thoughts, feelings or actions, can be quite a challenge but is well worth being aware of and practising regularly.

We get fixated on ideas and agendas that we hang on to as if it would be a great threat if we were to let them go - as if our whole life depended on clinging to our beliefs, ideas and worldview.

In fact we are naturally used to letting go. We let go of each breath that we take – a receiving and a release. In nature, plants need to let go of their seeds if they are

33

to germinate. Young birds need to let go of any fear they have before taking their first flight.

To illustrate this further, let's look at how Indian farmers capture monkeys that are destroying their crops. The farmers cut a hole in the top of a coconut just large enough for a monkey to slide in its hand. They then place a banana inside the coconut. When the monkey reaches in to grasp the banana, his clenched fist is too big to slide back out of the hole. The monkey is then trapped because it doesn't want to let go.

In the same way, these things we're attached to are the very things that hold us back, even causing pain in our lives. The harder we attempt to cling on to our concepts, our past experiences, our wants and desires and our expectations of how things ought to be, the harder it is for us to be fully present.

5. TRUSTING YOURSELF

Start the process of trusting ourselves and our intuition. It is preferable to trust ourselves in this way and maybe make a few mistakes along the way than to trust some external authority.

If something doesn't feel right to you, learn to go with that feeling. Why should you discount your intuition just because some authority or people think differently?

We have no problem trusting that our heart will beat, our eyes will see or that we will breathe. Have the confidence to trust in your own abilities.

In our mindful lives, this is an important attitude to develop.

6. PATIENCE IS A VIRTUE

I remember hearing the story of a man who was watching the amazing transformation of a butterfly emerging from a chrysalis. It can be a long process and the man, thinking the butterfly was struggling to break free, eased it gently out of the chrysalis. The butterfly never recovered.

As a butterfly emerges from a chrysalis, there's a lengthy pause while fluid is pumped into its wings and the wings dry out enabling it to fly. The man's impatience had bypassed this vital part of the process.

In the same way, things often have to unfold in their own time however tempting it is to jump right on in. As we learn a new skill like mindfulness and meditation, can we allow the changes to take place at their own pace? Have we got the patience to persevere, even if we see no progress being made?

Gardeners know the art of patience more than most. They cannot rush Nature's way of going from seed sown to mature plant. It can be a lengthy process for which no shortcut exists. As we languish in the cold of winter, we are often impatient for the summer to arrive but we know that it will, given time.

So patience is being open to each moment as it happens, without judgment, trusting that the process is unfolding perfectly as it is.

7. NON-STRIVING

The attitude of non-striving encourages us to back off from striving for results and instead to place the focus on the here and now. Allow things to be held in awareness without trying to make anything happen. This is not easy as we all have agendas and long 'To Do' lists!

It is engendering a different way, seeing whatever is going on in our lives right now this second as good enough, even though it might not feel that way. We don't have to try and avoid it, fix it or make anything happen. It doesn't mean that nothing gets done but it does happen out of being and not doing.

This does not infer that we should not set goals. Humans are goal-orientated. For example, if we set off to go on a walk in an unknown area to a place 15 miles away, we will, by necessity, check out how we're going to get there. This will entail mapping out the route in a series of goals to achieve in order to reach our destination.

By focusing on and accepting the present moment, with patience and regular practice, movement towards our goals will take place by itself.

8. COUNTING YOUR BLESSINGS

It's easy to see everything that's not right about our lives. On the other hand, if we look for it, there is a lot to be grateful for. The roof over our heads, our warm home, this morning's sunrise, our comfortable bed, food in the fridge, a loving spouse, friends at college, our health and so on. Don't forget the little things in life that we're grateful for, like, for instance, our reading glasses.

By being grateful we're giving heartfelt thanks all the time for what we **do** have rather than concentrating on what we don't have. This can lead to a seismic shift in our thinking, well-being and improved relationships.

At the end of every day, write down three things that you've been grateful for in the course of that day. Feeling the emotion of the gratitude you're expressing makes it more real.

9. ADOPTING A GIVING MENTALITY

When we stop thinking about ourselves and begin to focus on the needs of others, we take ourselves out of our own little world and begin to experience what it's like walking in someone else's shoes.

When we start to give our time, care and attention to others, we begin to feel not only a great sense of empathy and warmth inside but also we open ourselves up to reciprocal love.

Giving is not something that we do because we want people to notice how generous we are. That would just be feeding and growing the ego, the very thing that we're looking to see diminish.

5. THE FEEL GOOD FACTOR

*"Stay in the moment. The practice of staying present will heal
you. Obsessing about how the future will turn out creates
anxiety. Replaying broken scenarios from the past causes anger
and sadness. Stay here, in this moment"*
SYLVESTER MCNUTT

Before we go deeper into mindfulness exercises, let's take a look at what a mindfulness routine can do for our body and mind. But first we need to find our 'WHY'.

Why am I doing this? Why is it important to me? Without a strong enough *'Why',* we may find it harder to keep on track and start wandering from the main path. Some of the reasons why we want to start down the mindfulness road may be found in the list below or we may have compelling personal reasons. The more inspiring our reason, the more we're going to persevere. Think for a moment how you're going to feel when that new habit you're going to form becomes a reality? How will you feel when you become that happier, more peaceful person who is better able to manage crises and remain calm.

When we write our reasons 'Why' on a sticky Post-It and attach it to the fridge door, we can always refer to it when we need to. This helps enormously when those setbacks occur. We'll be having an in-depth look at obstacles later.

OK, so let's check out some of the amazing benefits we'll experience when we start practising mindfulness:

Mindfulness helps reduce anxiety and stress

There has been an enormous shift in how professionals view mindfulness in recent times. Mainstream health institutions are now recommending mindfulness. Psychotherapists now use mindfulness meditation to treat a number of mental health issues such as depression and insomnia.

Mindfulness improves other psychosomatic problems.

Problems such as eating disorders, relationship conflicts, obsessive-compulsive disorders and substance abuse are being tackled by the use of mindfulness within the health community.

Mindfulness improves sleep

It has been conclusively shown that mindful meditation reduces the amount of cortisol, the hormone associated with stress. It also increases melatonin, the hormone that acts on receptors in your body to encourage sleep.

Mindfulness lowers blood pressure

Relaxing in the form of meditation increases the formation of a compound, nitric oxide, which helps to widen blood vessels to allow more blood flow.

Mindfulness enhances sex lives

Research published in 2011 in the journal Psychosomatic Medicine concluded that mindfulness meditation training can enhance a woman's sexual experience by lowering the amount of judgmental internal chatter during sex which gives rise to a more satisfying experience.

Mindfulness eases aches and pains

A study in the April issue of the Journal of Neuroscience corroborated another study at the University of Montreal that just 80 minutes of mindful meditation could cut pain perception by nearly half.

Mindfulness improves decision making

A UCLA study in 2012 found that long-term meditators have more gyrification or folding of the brain's cortex than people who don't, which allows them to process information faster because they avoid ruminating on past events.

Mindfulness helps us to become more focused and improves our attention span

The actual act of focusing is enhanced by mindful meditation because while meditating this is what you're doing – dismissing unwanted thoughts while you concentrate on a specific activity like breathing. The 2008 brain scan study published in the journal Plos One concluded that even focusing on boring and repetitive tasks improved significantly.

Mindfulness improves moods

Marines who took part in a study practised mindful meditation for a period of two months and a radical improvement occurred to their moods and working memory, positively affecting their performance.

Mindfulness helps us to feel more empathy for others

A study published in 2008 in the journal Plos One showed that experienced and non-experienced meditators practising compassionate meditation, similar to that practised by Tibetan leaders, showed an increase in empathy.

Mindfulness reduces loneliness.

It helps us to become engaged with life and more connected with friends, family and people in general.

Mindfulness slows down neuro-degenerative diseases

Alzheimer's patients who took part in a pilot study at Beth Israel Deaconess Medical Centre showed a reduction in cognitive decline after an 8 week mindfulness-based stress reduction programme compared to another group that did not take part in it.

Which ones above resonate with you?

THE SCIENCE OF MINDFULNESS

Scientists are continuing to make discoveries about how meditation on its own can have such a healing effect on our minds and bodies. As we have seen already, meditation is nothing new – it has been around for 2,000 years - and the psychological benefits have not been scientifically known but have only come to light since we have begun to understand the inner workings of the mind more clearly.

In someone who does not meditate, the part of the brain that deals with self-consciousness and our interactions with others (the medial prefrontal cortex or 'self' centre), is more strongly connected to the parts of our brain that deal with sensation and fear. That means that the part of our brain that deals with reasoning and regulating emotional responses – the lateral prefrontal cortex - is weak.

However, someone who meditates will find that that the rational assessment centre is far stronger and is able override automatic behaviours. The 'self' centre and its connection with fear and sensation is weakened. This is how anxiety is reduced and how there is a more measured response to perceived threats.

6. MEDITATION AND MINDFULNESS EXERCISES

"The moment one gives close attention to anything, even a blade of grass, it becomes a mysterious, awesome, indescribably magnificent world in itself"

HENRY MILLER

MINDFULNESS MEDITATION TECHNIQUES

It is important that you have a calm environment in order to practice mindfulness. You do not want to be interrupted during your practice time so in order to do that you could wake up earlier than you normally do to ensure that you're able to practice undisturbed. By choosing a time first thing in the morning, you are less likely to be interrupted by people calling on the landline, visitors arriving at your door, Facebook notifications and the like. If this is not possible, it is well worth talking to those in your household and explaining that you will be needing however many minutes each morning when you do not wish to be disturbed. Switch off your mobile phone.

I would recommend you start your morning meditation exercise with the Complete Breath, which is known in yoga as 'pranayama'.

Why?

An ancient yoga text proclaims: "Life is in the Breath". We know this is self-evident in that you need to continuously breathe in order to stay alive. We also know that it is possible to survive for some time without food or water but it is difficult to survive more than a few minutes without breathing.

However, the Complete Breath is much more than simply supplying oxygen to our lungs and then into our blood stream. If anyone is suffering from fatigue, frequent headaches, anxiety, poor circulation, a below-par complexion, nervousness, is easily upset or has an unsettled mind, the Yogi will firstly look at their breathing and assess whether it is shallow, partial or erratic. So many physical and mental problems today can be traced back to faulty respiration.

This type of deep breathing lowers our heart rate, increases energy, detoxifies the body and improves digestion to name just a few of the ways we can benefit from this exercise. But the Complete Breath is more than just deep breathing. We can breathe deeply but still not fill our lungs completely. This practice consists of filling the lower, middle and upper chambers of the lungs in a rhythmic fashion to obtain the maximum well-being.

This technique will take around three minutes.

You may prefer not to start with The Complete Breath and that's absolutely fine. Skip the next section if that's what you choose but I would recommend that at some point you incorporate this into your daily practice.

THE COMPLETE BREATH

Dress in loose clothing and dispense with tightly fitting belts. Sit in any position that you find comfortable. If you sit cross-legged on the floor, place a yoga block or a cushion under your buttocks. You can sit with a straight back on a chair with your feet on the floor, hands on your thighs and looking straight ahead although you can perform this exercise with your eyes closed. Remove any tension in your body and face muscles and just breathe normally for a few moments.

All breathing is very slow and very quiet and ensure that all movements flow into each other. Perform 3 times. All breathing is done through the nose.

Practice pushing out (distending) your abdomen and then contracting it. These are the two specific movements that you'll be using in this exercise.

So to begin the exercise, slowly exhale breathe through your nose and at the same time contract your abdomen until there is no breath left in your lungs. Then begin slowly to inhale air while simultaneously distending your abdomen allowing oxygen to fill the lower chamber of your lungs.

As you continue inhaling, contract your abdomen slightly as you expand your chest as much as you can. When you think your chest cannot take much more air, slowly raise your shoulders as high as possible allowing air to reach your upper lungs. Hold your breath for a count of 5. Very slowly exhale and let your body relax.

Repeat the movements.

MINDFULNESS MEDITATION

After the Complete Breath, look to meditate intentionally for five minutes in the beginning. You can start at one minute and then build upon that during your first week until you reach five minutes. If you feel able to meditate longer, then that's fine – whatever you feel most comfortable with.

Studies have found that meditating for 25-30 minutes will give the greatest benefits so look to that as a goal to attain longer term. The amount of time you spend on this is not important at this stage. What *is* important is getting into the habit of doing it every day or at least 5 days a week. **Jon Kabat-Zinn's advice to beginners is that you don't have to enjoy meditation. Just commit to it and the benefits will unfold in due course.**

You can carry straight on from the Complete Breath into this next exercise.

Set the alarm function on your mobile ensuring the sound of the alarm is set to low volume and is relaxing. If you prefer, have a clock within view but it can be too distracting when you find yourself looking at it every so often.

1. An upright chair is best to maintain an erect spine. Avoid armchairs and recliners. Rest your hands on your thighs or the arms of the chair.

2. You can either close your eyes altogether or lower your gaze so it falls unfocused on the floor a metre or so from your feet.

3. Allow your body and facial muscles to relax but stay aware and alert.

4. Now begin to concentrate on your normal breathing. Become aware of the rising and falling of your diaphragm; the cool air entering your nostrils and the warm air on the out-breath; the rising and falling of the ribcage.

5. After five minutes or so, open your eyes and become aware of your surroundings again

It's normal for the mind to wander all over the place. Accept this as part of the process. Don't be hard on yourself when this happens.

As the mind begins to wander, observe the thought, accept it and let it go without judging yourself or being in any way critical of your actions. If another thought comes to mind, again accept it and let it go again and refocus on your breathing.

OTHER MINDFULNESS MEDITATION
TECHNIQUES

You can look at incorporating these techniques into your meditation plan as an extra or to get some variety into your routines. It's a good idea to record your experiences in a good Meditation/Mindfulness Journal (see page 91) to see the progress you are making.

BODY SCAN MEDITATION

This can be done in a sitting position or lying on the floor for 15 – 30 minutes. If sitting, use a high-back chair for support, with your hands on your thighs.

If you decide to lie down, you can do so on your bed, a yoga mat or a rug so that you are comfortable. Draw up your knees with your feet on the bed/floor. Use a pillow if you wish for comfort.

Keep your eyes closed but you can open them if you feel sleepy. If you do fall asleep, don't judge yourself. If it continues, then try sitting in a chair next time.

The purpose of this exercise is to start at your feet and scan your body slowly, working your way up to your head, focusing on each part of your body as you do so. During this exercise, let go of any unwanted thoughts. Don't judge yourself for having them. This is perfectly natural. Just let them go and continue focusing on your scan.

In certain parts of your anatomy, you may well be aware of tension, stiffness, heaviness and so on. You may be aware of them but do not judge or react.

Start with your left toes and feet, including the sole and heel. What sensations do you feel – the touch of one toe on another or tingling maybe?

Work your way up to your shins, knees and thighs spending about 30 seconds on each area and then concentrate on the right leg and repeat.

Next, focus your attention on the region of the genitals, buttocks and hips taking your time again over each area. Then focus on your lower back and your abdomen noticing as it rises and falls with your breathing. Then your upper back and chest where you'll be aware of the rising and falling of your ribcage as you breathe. Can you feel your heart beating?

Now bring your attention to the thumb and fingers of your left hand, then the palm, wrist and the back and sides of the hand. Going up the left arm, focus on the lower arm, elbow, upper arm and shoulder. Repeat with the right arm starting at the thumb and fingers.

Next, be aware of your throat and neck. Then move your jaw and feel your lips move apart and come together. How does this feel? With your tongue, feel your teeth, gums and palate.

Be aware of your eyes and eyelids. Feel the blinking and what happens when you do so.

At your nose, experience the inhalations and exhalations. Is there a difference in temperature in your nostrils between an in-breath and an out-breath?

Next, focus on your cheeks, temple and forehead followed by the back of your head and scalp including your hair against your skin.

Finish the exercise by being aware of your entire body and in particular, your breath as it gives life to your entire being. Be kind to yourself. Offer up some self-love as you thank yourself for taking the time to appreciate your body.

OBJECT MEDITATION

So far we've concentrated on the breath and the body. Now we'll look at concentrating our attention on an object. Eastern meditation focus is often a candle flame. We're going to use all our five senses in turn wherever we are able. Choose an object, artificial or natural that you can handle. Spend 5 – 15 minutes observing the object carefully. By using a fruit, for example, you can finish the practice by eating it.

When teaching his Mindfulness-Based Stress Reduction Programme, Jon Kabat-Zinn uses a raisin to teach his classes object based meditation. What he was getting at here was that meditation isn't something lofty in the sense that it's above real life but more of a closer engagement with it.

A FRUIT - Take a fruit of your choice.

First, hold the object in the palm of your hand.

Explore its colour – is it the same across all the surface?

Are there any irregularities on the skin? Is it shiny or dull?

Is the surface rough or smooth?

Does it feel warm or cold?

Bringing the fruit to your nose, does it have a fragrance?

When you take a bite, what is its texture in your mouth?

What does it taste like?

A LEAF - Natural objects are ideal for this type of meditation. You can try things like leaves, shells, conkers, feathers, pebbles, flowers and ears of wheat. For example if you choose a leaf, hold it in the palm of your hand.

How does it feel in your hand?

Does it sit flat on your palm or does it touch some parts of your hand but not others?

Is it warm or cold?

Is its temperature changing the longer you hold it?

Does it feel rough or smooth?

Is it firm or limp, damp or dry?

What are edges of the leaf shaped like?

Is the leaf the same colour on both sides or is there a variation?

Is it blemished in any way?

What pattern is there on the leaf?

Holding the leaf to your nose, what does it smell like? Can you compare the smell to anything?

In the beginning, you may find it difficult to keep your thoughts under control. That's OK. Don't be hard on yourself. This is a new discipline for you to understand and everyone is very different. The one common thread in all this – and I cannot stress this enough - is not to quit but to keep to a regular habit to see the maximum change in your life.

MINDFULNESS AT WORK

For many of us, work signifies a place where we may be under more stress than in any other environment in our day-to-day lives. It is important for our mental well-being that we can find a place at work where we can sit undisturbed and practice mindfulness meditation for 3 minutes. It will depend on your circumstances at work. In a quiet office environment, this practice could take place at your work station; in a more frenetic atmosphere, then retiring to the restroom could be an option or even a toilet cubicle.

This can be done when you're feeling overly stressed - things have got on top of you and you may be at your wits end. For example, your breathing has increased, the muscles in your neck and shoulders are aching and your hands are sweating. You are feeling completely overwhelmed and need to calm down.

You may want to incorporate the following exercise into your day and do it 2-3 times during your working hours to maintain your equilibrium or, alternatively, use it as and when you need to. You can set your phone to mute and the alarm for 3 minutes

Choose a seated position and close or lower your eyes. Concentrate on your breathing. Feel the air as it enters your nostrils and as you exhale. Keep your focus entirely on your breathing. If the mind wanders, gently and without judgment let go of that thought and bring your attention back to the breathing.

Breathing never happens in the past or the future. It's always happening now in the present moment. You will find this exercise greatly improves your overall well-being.

Three minutes is enough time to calm the limbic part of your brain that deals with emotions and engage the reasoning part. In these circumstances, your mind needs a rest and the space to assimilate what's going on externally as well as internally. No conscious effort is required because the brain will do this itself behind the scenes.

You might like to try a shortened version of the above exercise at your workstation lasting just one minute. Even though it's a very short exercise, you will still notice a difference.

WALKING MINDFULNESS

For many people, walking gives them a chance to ponder on any worries and anxieties they are experiencing and gives them the opportunity to find ways to resolve them.

To walk mindfully means that we put those issues to one side. If the mind starts to focus on them, we calmly and non-judgmentally let those thoughts go. To be mindful is to be aware of the present moment in every situation including when you are in the great outdoors.

Just as you can be mindful when folding freshly laundered clothes or while you attend to DIY jobs around your home, so you can stimulate your senses by walking mindfulness.

There is no particular technique when it comes to walking mindfulness. What we want to achieve is focusing on what is around us – what we can see, hear, smell, touch or taste. Of course your mind will want to pry you away with numerous and varied thoughts if you allow it to. Let go of any thoughts that crop up. Remember not to judge yourself or beat yourself up for having those thoughts. Continue to nurture your appreciation for the place in which you find yourself.

Listen to the songbirds singing their hearts out and feel the warmth of the sun's rays upon your exposed flesh. In the summer, pick some juicy, tasty blackberries. What does the berry feel like in your hand? Are there any imperfections in the fruit? What does it taste like?

If the weather is inclement, feel the rain on your face or listen to your boots as they crunch through fresh snow. Smell the fragrance of summer flowers by the side of the path or the wafting of smoke from wood burning stoves.

While walking around museums or churches, what smells do you notice? Pay close attention to everything you see and hear more so than you've ever done before.

Check out the characters and colours of stained glass windows. Take special interest in museum exhibits.

When entering shops, listen to the conversations of other people without judging what they're saying. Be aware of what's being sold – the shapes, colours, smells of the materials. What do the products feel like? How do the styles differ?

Outside in the street, listen to the cars and buses. What smells are you getting from the various shops? Check out the buildings. When you look up at the upper storeys of buildings what do you notice?

The mind is constantly pushing its agenda on to you – all those things **it** wants **you** to focus on but you just let go of all that stuff in your head that is vying for your attention. It's really all about focusing on your senses within any given environment and if the mind wanders, to accept the thought for what it is, let go of it and bring your attention back to the present moment – the here and now.

7. OBSTACLES AND HOW TO OVERCOME THEM

"Peace of mind is not the absence of conflict from life, but the ability to cope with it"
ANONYMOUS

As we have already seen, mindfulness is not just for when we sit down and meditate. It's best practised throughout our day wherever we happen to be. As we tune in to our immediate surroundings and start to take notice of what is around us, we start to appreciate more of what we are experiencing. Our minds become more connected to the present moment and the constant chatter of the mind is silenced.

However, right at the very start of our journey even though we may know that this practice is going to benefit our lives hugely, we may find reasons not to do

69

it. As we have already seen, the subconscious mind is keen to maintain the status quo. It does not like change. So any resistance to change is natural and can be expected. Having a strong 'Why' – why we want to embark on this journey – is so crucial to starting and maintaining mindfulness practice.

In this chapter we'll be looking at obstacles that we're likely to face along the way.

1. I DON'T HAVE ANY TIME – This is usually associated with the practice of mindfulness meditation which requires a certain amount of time set aside every day. Unless you make mindfulness meditation a daily routine, it may well not happen at all. I would challenge anyone who says they have no time to spend, say, ten minutes meditating.

How much time do we devote to media in the course of one day? In 2019 the average time per day that people spent on social media worldwide was 2 hours 24 minutes. Add to that the time we spend watching TV, YouTube, vlogs, gaming and visiting websites, you can see that time is available. It depends on what you want to prioritise in your life.

2. I CAN'T FIND A QUIET PLACE IN MY HOME – Again, this refers to the meditation side of our practice. This can be challenging especially if, say, you're house-sharing as a student with a number of adults in the same home. Pressures can mount with family homes where young children are up at the break of dawn demanding a feed. The Covid-19 pandemic of 2020 has exacerbated the situation with enforced lockdowns.

If you know folk in your home rise at a certain time try setting the alarm earlier than you would normally do. Mornings are typically the best time for meditation because it tends to set you up for the rest of the day. On saying that, if it's just not possible to find a quiet place early in the morning, consider meditating at other times of the day when you can have access to an undisturbed session.

3.   MY MIND JUST WON'T SLOW DOWN – This can be related to meditation practice and mindfulness in general. You may have spent your entire life with your mind in control of **you**. It's going to take practice to reverse this trend.   Using natural patterns, such as breathing, work really well because it gives something for your mind to dwell on wherever you are. Ensure that with meditation practice you have turned off all external sources of noise such as your mobile, TV, computer etc. Don't worry if you seem to make no headway in your first sessions. As with anything in life, the more you persevere, the more you'll see the rewards.

It's so important to remember not to beat yourself up if you find sessions difficult or even impossible. **The most important piece of advice I can give is to maintain mindfulness meditation practice every day for 60 days even if you see no difference at all initially.**

This enables a habit to be formed. It will mean that you are less likely to be resisting the notion of mindful meditation and it will be something you naturally do without thinking too much about it. In these days of instant gratification where we all want immediate results, you need to ensure that our 'Why' is strong enough.

4. MY PROGRESS IS NOT FAST ENOUGH – Remember that mindfulness is not a race. Pushing for progress is likely to be counterproductive. I would reiterate what I said above in that to change the habit of a lifetime is going to take time. Every mindful moment that you incorporate into your daily life will be making a difference. Mindfulness is a practice unconcerned with 'producing results'. It is focused on *being* and *non*-doing.

5. I'M BEGINNING TO DOUBT – One of the reasons we never achieve our full potential in life can be put down to this pesky little voice in the back of our minds telling us "I can't handle this", "I'll never get the hang of it" or "I've never been any good at this sort of thing". Doubt comes from an inner belief we have about our ability to do something or handle something. It's the result of fear and resistance and it is very common.

Go back to your 'Why' – your reasons for embarking on this mindfulness journey. I imagine your reasons will be something like wanting to increase your inner peace, finding more calm amidst difficult situations, being better able to focus, improving anxiety and stress levels.

The problems and challenges you face are teachers in disguise. Listen to what your own obstacles are trying to tell you. Begin to practice recognising the setback for what it is, accepting its presence and then letting it go. They don't have to hold you captive unless you allow them to. It's simple in theory but not quite so easy in practice initially.

6. MY MIND SEEMS SO RESTLESS – You may be susceptible to a flurry of thoughts, physical sensations and emotions. There may be a sense of being distracted, irritable and in a state where you cannot keep still for long. It is in these sorts of mental disturbances that you would benefit from mindfulness the most.   Sit down and fully concentrate on your breathing. Just doing this for a few minutes will have the effect of calming your mind.

7. I SUFFER FROM CHRONIC PAIN – Chronic pain means you are likely to have more stress in your life than people who don't.   Therefore pain is stressful. Having pain may mean that you are able to do less in your life and this can create stress. Tighter muscles, lack of sleep, shallow breathing, anxiety, a depressed mood are all associated with stress and all of these can lead to worse pain. **Pain flares are fuelled by stress**. Learn to reduce the stress and you may need less medication.

Pain = unpleasant physical reaction + your physical, cognitive (thinking, understanding) and emotional reactions to the sensation.

Here's a 5 minute exercise for you:

During your mindfulness meditation practice, firstly keep your focus as much as you can on your body and breathing. Some present-moment sensations may be pleasant; others, such as the pain, may be unpleasant. Accept your experience just as it is without needing to change or improve anything.

Imagine your mind is like the sky and the pain is like a cloud.

Scan your entire body from your feet to your head observing each area as you go.

Once you have completed this, focus on your breathing. Feel your rib cage rising and falling with each breath.

Count 'one' on your first out-breath. On your second out-breath count 'two' and so on up to 'ten'. When you reach 'ten', start again at 'one'.

It has been found repeatedly that those who complete an eight week mindfulness programme find that their pain is relieved.

8. MY MIND KEEPS WANDERING – This is perfectly natural and we have mentioned this a number of times so far. This is what your mind has been doing for years and years. It has been able to go from one thought to another at will and as we've already seen, one thought can lead to many others until we have a whole string of them.

With mindfulness, the aim is to bring your mind under your control and not to let it take off in any number of directions. It has had its own way and like a spoilt child, it won't give in without a little effort on your part.

The mind is basically like a muscle. The more you exercise a muscle, the stronger it gets. People who consistently visit gyms twice a week start to see a big difference in their overall body weight and muscle tone in a relatively short space of time. The mind is no different. It needs to be exercised by performing mindfulness techniques but as I've stated previously, one or two days of practice is not going to make much difference to your overall well-being.

Sometimes we can be doing walking meditation and a thought comes into our minds about something that is fairly important to us and it demands to be kept in mind lest we forget. This can take our focus clean away from the present moment and into the future. 'If I don't get this bill paid today, then the bank will start charging interest'. No matter what you do, that thought can be with you till you get home.

Carrying a small, pocket notebook can help defuse these situations. Jot the pressing problem down in your notebook and continue on using your five senses in the here and now and putting that thought to bed until you are able to deal with it. Always be aware that a wandering mind is natural and doesn't mean you're doing anything wrong. With regular practice, this will lessen in intensity.

9. I FEEL SLEEPY – It's difficult when you're tired to be alert and aware of the present moment. There is *actual* physical fatigue and then there is *resistance* to something that's going on in your mind or body. When you are experiencing fearful or painful emotions, the body reacts to this internal resistance in the form of sleepiness. You need to check out which of these two you are dealing with.

Meditating after a long, exhausting day at work is not recommended. Your mind and your body allocate their energy needs based upon the most important physiological needs and, in this case, recovering your energy through sleep is your most pressing priority.

When fearful or painful emotions are causing the sleepiness, concentrate on your breathing so that this becomes your predominant present moment activity.

Wherever you can, try and complete your meditation early in the morning if this is possible in your situation.

10. I HAVE AN ADDICTIVE BEHAVIOUR – Addiction is an attachment to pleasure that ensnares us in an automatic programme that continually feeds our desires. It becomes a desperate struggle as we become increasingly mindless pursuing more of what we can't get enough of. Dopamine swamps our system as we surrender to our addiction which makes this self-sustaining cycle more difficult to escape from.

Overriding this conditioned behaviour can only be done through diligent practice as mindful awareness begins to gain control. Sometimes, a course of counselling may be the best option, depending on how severe the addiction is.

11. I FEEL OVERWHELMED - This can be due to a number of negative and disempowering reasons going on at the same time eliciting a feeling of overwhelm and just too much on your mind to cope with. The stress of the situation is what needs to be addressed.

Acknowledge and accept the feeling of being overwhelmed or stressed.

This does not mean you have to accept problematic or stressful situations as a norm. It means accepting the way you feel about things in a given moment before handling the situation. What is happening may not be pleasant, but by accepting it and not resisting it, you engage the neocortex or reasoning part of your brain that deals with thinking and finding solutions.

And breathe…..

The great thing about this is that we can practice it at anytime and anywhere by taking time-out from what we're doing and focusing on our breathing for just 2-3 minutes.

8. LOOKING AHEAD

"Surrender to what is.
Let go of what was.
Have faith in what will be."
SONIA RICOTTI

I said at the very start of this book that, with mindfulness, we're on a journey and, together, we have explored along the way what mindfulness is, delving a little into its history, examining brain and mind functions, getting involved in actual exercises and looking at the obstacles and ways to defeat them.

We have seen that diligently practising the exercises outlined in this book can have a transformative effect on our lives. Our lives can be enriched with more happiness, peace and joy than we ever thought possible.

Everything you need to heal yourself is within you.

You do not have to go looking for the latest fad or some expensive course to alleviate anxiety, depression and ailments of all kinds. By practising all that you've learnt in this book, you'll be on your way to a more fulfilled and contented life

The strange thing is, we can know all these things and still decide not to go ahead. We can give mental assent to the techniques and benefits and can see how people's lives can be improved, but decide that it's not for us.

How about you?

I believe that you have a different mindset. After all, you've made it to the end of this book. Statistically, when it comes to reading books, not many people do that!

Make a promise to yourself that you will practice for the next 60 days to make mindfulness a habit in your life. Sixty days is no time at all in the great scheme of things. It doesn't matter what crops up to tempt you off the path (and it will!), you know how to deal with it and you **will** finish. Things won't always go to plan.

Accept the hindrance for what it is and restart the next day if necessary. Remember to have fun while you progress on this journey of discovery.

You've got what it takes.

You know what to do.

AND FINALLY.....

I do hope that you enjoyed this book and that you would be happy to recommend it to others.

By leaving a review on Amazon, you would help me so much to get the message out there to a larger audience and for them to experience a calmer and more worry-free life too.

If you would like to contact me, then I would love to hear from you – grahamcann6@gmail.com

Thank you.

Graham

DO YOU LIKE READING BOOKS?

WOULD YOU LIKE US TO SEND YOU **FREE** BOOKS?

Chas Cann Publishers would love you to join our Advance Readers Club.

All members receive free e-books on all sorts of interesting subjects which have included puppy care, cookbooks, joke books and mindfulness.

You will receive a copy prior to the book being published and marketed globally.

All we ask you to do is to read it and then leave an honest review on Amazon.

Go to info@chascannco.com to be added to our VIP list of readers.

Also available from the publisher of this book:

Just scan the QR code to find out more

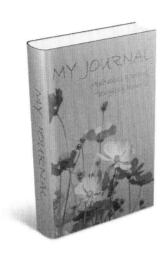

My Journal' is designed with YOU in mind, and is for your Meditations, Dreams, Thoughts and Memories.

This **UNIQUE**, beautifully illustrated journal has been especially created to inspire you, relieve your stress, and help you to reflect and record your special memories.

Inside all pages include thought provoking and motivational quotes designed to boost your mood, inspire creativity and empower you to achieve your dreams in life.

Take time to relax, reflect and express your inner feelings within this notebook, to keep and treasure always.

What you will LOVE about 'My Journal':
- 150 pages of quality paper perfect for gel pen, ink or pencils
- Each page has an image of delightful spring flowers
- Perfect gift for Christmas and birthdays
- Value for money
- Elegant personal diary
- Connect to your inner peaceful self
- Ideal size to carry with you everywhere in your bag

Known BENEFITS of Journaling:
- Journaling is known to improve your mental health and well-being
- Increases working memory capacity
- Inspires creativity

- Helps to organise your thoughts
- Allows you to focus on what you are grateful for
- Helps you to prioritize problems and daily dilemmas

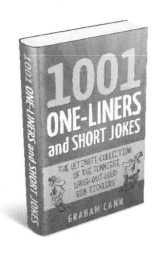

They're all here in this classic collection of the most hilarious one-liners on planet Earth!

This eye-watering compilation has been carefully selected to get your giggle glands going and is guaranteed to give you hours of laughter and enjoyment.

Each of the 1001 gags has been placed into one of over 40 categories such as Women, Religion, Politics and Sex so that you can find a joke easily on any number of topics.

A wise sage once said, "Laughter is, and will always be, the best form of therapy" so go on, cheer yourself up with this fabulous collection of mirth and merriment.

Ideal as a birthday gift or stocking filler.

Enter a magical creative world that puts you in control and reconnect to your inner creativity.

'Colour 'N Relax' your stress away with these beautifully illustrated, intricate and diverse designs.

Discover inspiring quotes to muse over while you take time out of your busy day to colour your way to peace and calm.

◆ **150 pages** of detailed, varied designs catering for all levels of artistic creativity, including uplifting quotes to inspire and motivate.

◆ **Intricate illustrations** of mandalas, flowers, swirling patterns and so much more designed to exercise your imagination.

◆ **The ideal alternative** to too much screen time. Lose yourself as you focus your mind while you colour away your stress and anxiety.

◆ **Slow down and relax**. Feel that tension melt away as you colour and rediscover your creativity.

◆ **Ideal gift** for Mothers' Day, Birthdays, Easter and Vacations.

Have you been trying to lose weight but no amount of dieting seems to help?

You may have completed a diet but have you been unable to maintain that weight?

Are mood swings getting the better of your mental health?

Is lack of energy preventing you from living the life you want to live?

Jane Oliver has experienced the incredible health benefits of following the ketogenic lifestyle and has compiled her favourite go-to recipes in one place to help you look good and feel great.

The Keto Diet Cookbook is a compact and concise guide that points the way to totally transforming your physical and mental well-being in no time at all. It is ideal for beginners.

This FULLY UPDATED AND IMPROVED 3RD EDITION includes desserts, US measurements and so much more.

The Keto Diet Cookbook is your one-stop guide for weight loss and well-being.

If you like eating well and living life to the full, then you'll love Jane Oliver's life changing Keto Diet Cookbook.

<u>This is what customers are saying about this book:</u>

"This is a wonderful addition to the kitchen library!........This is a great reference for some quick weeknight meals which is an added bonus! It makes it so easy to stick to this diet" ★★★★★

"Perfect for a beginner or more advanced cook" ★★★★★

"This little book is full of great ideas with delicious recipes. Good variety. Well written and easy to use" ★★★★★

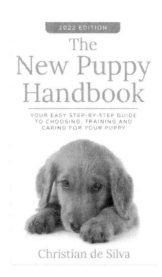

"The New Puppy Handbook is the only book you'll ever need for raising a healthy and well-behaved puppy"

When you've made the decision to introduce a puppy into your home, you may be naturally apprehensive, particularly if you are becoming pet parents for the first time.

Many let doubts and indecision stand in the way of what is such a challenging but rewarding experience. This is due mainly to potential pet owners not having the correct information in the first place.

As with anything in life, it's easier when you know how!

This detailed, comprehensive step-by-step guide to choosing, owning and caring for your puppy will be all that you need. By following and putting into practice what you read in this book, your puppy will become a happy and well-adjusted adult canine and you will become the most confident pet owner you can possibly be.

INSIDE:

Choosing a Suitable Breed

Finding Reputable Puppy Breeders

Budgeting for your Puppy

Shopping for Supplies and Equipment

Puppy Proofing your Home and Garden

Training

And so much more…………..